Johannes Brahms
(1833–1897)

Scherzo, Balladen, Rhapsodien und Tänze

für Klavier · for piano · pour piano

Urtext

Herausgegeben von · Edited by · Edité par
Enikő Gyenge
K 116
Könemann Music Budapest

INDEX

Scherzo, Op. 4

5

4 Balladen, Op. 10

Op. 10, No. 1

19

Op. 10, No. 2

22

Intermezzo, Op. 10, No. 3

28

Op. 10, No. 4

32

2 Rhapsodien, Op. 79

Op. 79, No. 1

40

Op. 79, No. 2

48

16 Walzer, Op. 39

Originalfassung – Original Version – Version originale

Op. 39, No. 1

55

Op. 39, No. 2

56

Op. 39, No. 3

56

Op. 39, No. 4

57

Op. 39, No. 5

58

Op. 39, No. 6

58

Op. 39, No. 7

60

Op. 39, No. 8

61

Op. 39, No. 9

9. 

62

Op. 39, No. 10

10. 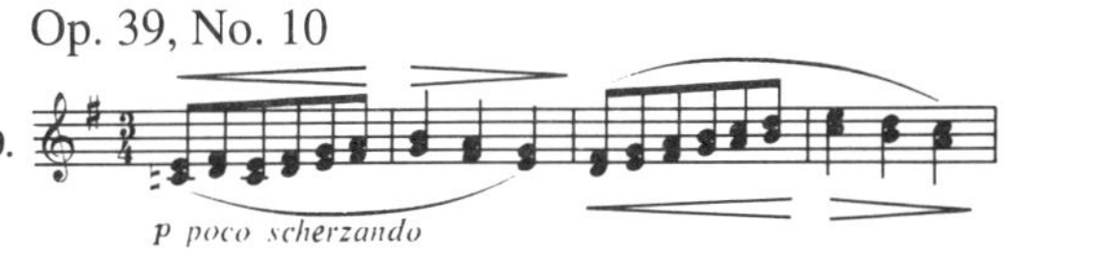

62

Op. 39, No. 11

11. 

63

Op. 39, No. 12

12. 

64

Op. 39, No. 13

13. 

65

Op. 39, No. 14

14. 

65

Op. 39, No. 15

15. 

67

Op. 39, No. 16

16. 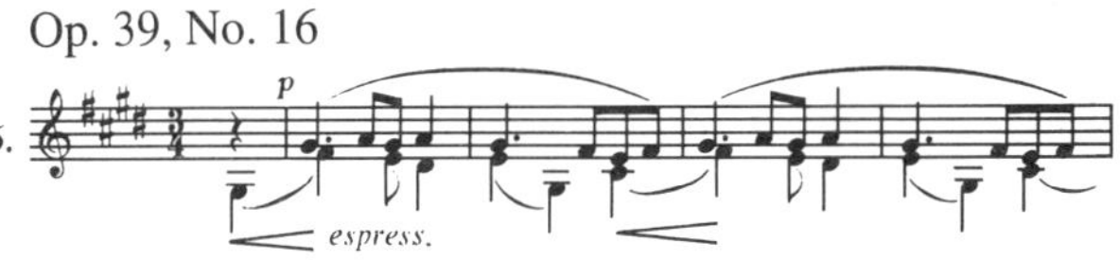

68

16 Walzer, Op. 39
Erleichterte Fassung – Facilitated Version – Version facilitée

Op. 39, No. 1

Tempo giusto

1. 

69

Op. 39, No. 2

2. 

70

Op. 39, No. 3

3. 

70

Op. 39, No. 4

Poco sostenuto

4. 

71

Op. 39, No. 5

Grazioso

5. 
72

Op. 39, No. 6

Vivace

6. 

72

Op. 39, No. 7

Poco più Andante

7. 

74

Op. 39, No. 8

8. 

75

Op. 39, No. 9

9. 

76

Op. 39, No. 10

10. 

76

Op. 39, No. 11

11. 

77

Op. 39, No. 12

12. 

78

Op. 39, No. 13

13. 

79

Op. 39, No. 14

14. 

79

Op. 39, No. 15

15. 

81

Op. 39, No. 16

16. 

82

10 Ungarische Tänze – Hungarian Dances – Danses Hongroises, WoO 1

WoO 1, No. 1

1. 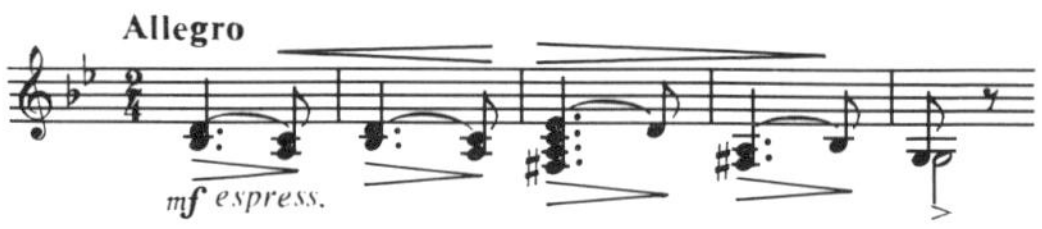

83

WoO 1, No. 2

2. 

88

WoO 1, No. 3

3. 

92

WoO 1, No. 4

4. 

96

WoO 1, No. 5

5. 

100

WoO 1, No. 6

6. 

104

WoO 1, No. 7

7. 

108

WoO 1, No. 8

8. 

110

WoO 1, No. 9

9. 

116

WoO 1, No. 10

10. 

118

Gavotte, WoO posth. 3, No. 1

121

2 Gigues, WoO posth. 4

WoO posth. 4, No. 1

1. 
122

WoO posth. 4, No. 2

2. 
124

2 Sarabanden, WoO posth. 5

WoO posth. 5, No. 1

1. 

126

WoO posth. 5, No. 2

2. 

127

Appendix
Gavotte, WoO posth. 3, No. 2

128

Notes 130

Ernst Ferdinand Wenzel zugeeignet

Scherzo

Op. 4
Hamburg, 1851

Rasch und feurig

staccato e leggiero
cresc.
leggiero
ben cantando ed espress.
legato
poco a poco cresc.
cresc.
ben marcato
poco a poco più
sostenuto
poco a

poco in tempo
78
sf
f
f
84
p
90
f
marcato
cresc.
96
cresc. e pesante
ff ben marcato
104
112
sff
ff

119
ff strepitoso
126
ben marcato
sf
ff
sf
8
135
8
144
8
1
Trio I
152
f
p
f
p e leggiero
scher-
161
zando
p

171
p
pp
p
pp
p
180
espressivo
più f
piacevole
pp
190
199
f
f
208
p
dolce
218
dim.
sost. poco

227
a tempo
p teneramente
237
poco sostenuto
a tempo
246
257
267
poco rf
legato e scherzando
277

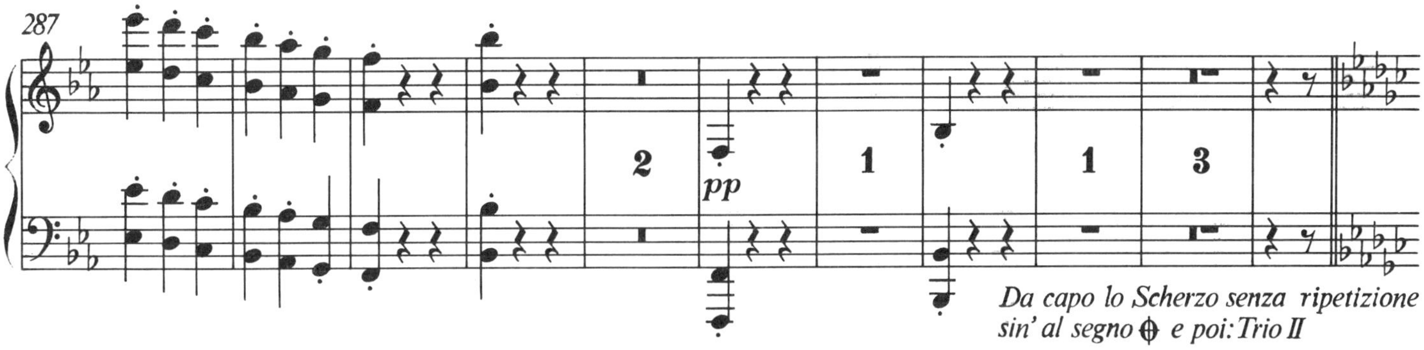
287
2
1
1
3
pp
Da capo lo Scherzo senza ripetizione
sin' al segno ⊕ e poi: Trio II

Trio II

Molto espressivo
301
f
Ped.
309
Ped.
317
f
324

331
poco sostenuto
cresc.
338
ff
Ped.
346
Ped.
354
sostenuto
f
p
dolce
360
sempre cresc.

366
cresc.
373
p
380
dolce
389
dim.
p e dolce con espress.
397
cresc.
403
f
f

410
ff
sempre
Ped.
418
più ff
8
426
8
ff
8
433
sostenuto
poco f
cresc.
442
ff
ff
Ped.

450
mf
457
p
ben marc.
463
f
471
f
m.s.
Ped.
marcato
Ped.
più f
Ped.
478
486
dim.
p
1
p
1

495
p
staccato e leggiero
cresc.
502
leggiero
p
p
ben cantando ed espress.
511
legato
poco a poco cresc.
521
cresc.
f
sf
ben marc.
poco a poco sostenuto
531
ff
sf

540
a tempo
sf
sf
f
p
547
dim.
f
554
cresc.
marcato
cresc. e
561
pesante
ff
ben marcato
570
sff
ff

579
ff strepitoso
586
ff ben marc.
poco a poco accelerando
594
602
Più mosso
610
Più sostenuto
619

Julius O. Grimm gewidmet

4 Balladen

Op. 10
Düsseldorf, 1854

Nach der schottischen Ballade: "Edward"
in Herders "Stimmen der Völker"

Op. 10, No. 1

Andante

Allegro (ma non troppo)

49
poco a poco riten. e
ff
sempre col Pedale
54
dimin.
rit.
Tempo I
p sotto
pp
60
voce
stacc. e p
pp
p
63
pp
67
p
dim. ma sempre in tempo

2.

Andante Op. 10, No. 2

28
f
Ped.
33
Ped.
38
cresc.
sf
ff
43
ff
47

molto staccato e leggiero
p
sf
pp legato

70
pp
75
p
80
f
85
Ped.
90
Ped.
95
cresc.
sf
sf ff
sf

100
ff
105
p
110
pp
dimin.
poco riten.
Ped.
Tempo I
Andante
118
p
espress.e dolce
legato
122
pp

127
p
131
136
p
espressivo
dolce
col Ped.
141
sempre riten. e dimin.
dim.
m.d.
145
riten.
pp

Intermezzo

Op. 10, No. 3

Allegro

3.

dim.
dolce
Ped.
pp
ppp

43
pp sempre legato
m.s.
51
pp
59
sempre in tempo
67
pp
75
dim.
ppp
84
pp

sempre pp molto leggiero
93
97
pp
102
dimin.
107
dolce
112
117
poco riten.
ppp
dim.
8

4.

Andante con moto Op. 10, No. 4

22
27
32
37
42
Ped.

Più lento
Col intimissimo sentimento, ma senza troppo marcare la melodia
47
pp
Ped.
49
Ped.
51
53
1.
54 b
2.
pp
dolce

56
58
dim.
60
62
64
cresc.
p

66
68
dim.
70
Tempo I
73
dolce
leggiero
legato
78

83
dim.
89
pp
96
102
sf
p
pp
espress.
108
cresc.
sf dimin.
p

115
123
130
Più lento
pp
mezza voce
col Ped.
136
138
p
dimin.

poco a poco riten. e dimin.
140
espress.
142
pp
144
146
riten.
Adagio

Frau Elisabeth von Herzogenberg gewidmet

2 Rhapsodien

Op. 79
Pörtschach, 1879

Op. 79, No. 1

24
p
30
pp
poco rit.
in tempo
35
f
40
p mezza voce
Ped.
45
cresc.
f
Ped.
Ped.
49
8
8
f

53
sf
sempre cresc.
57
8
ff
61
f
64
ff
fz
67

71
cresc.
75
79
più f
83
87
dim.
rit.

94
molto dolce espress.
col Ped.
98
102
1.
2.
105
cresc.
109
dim.

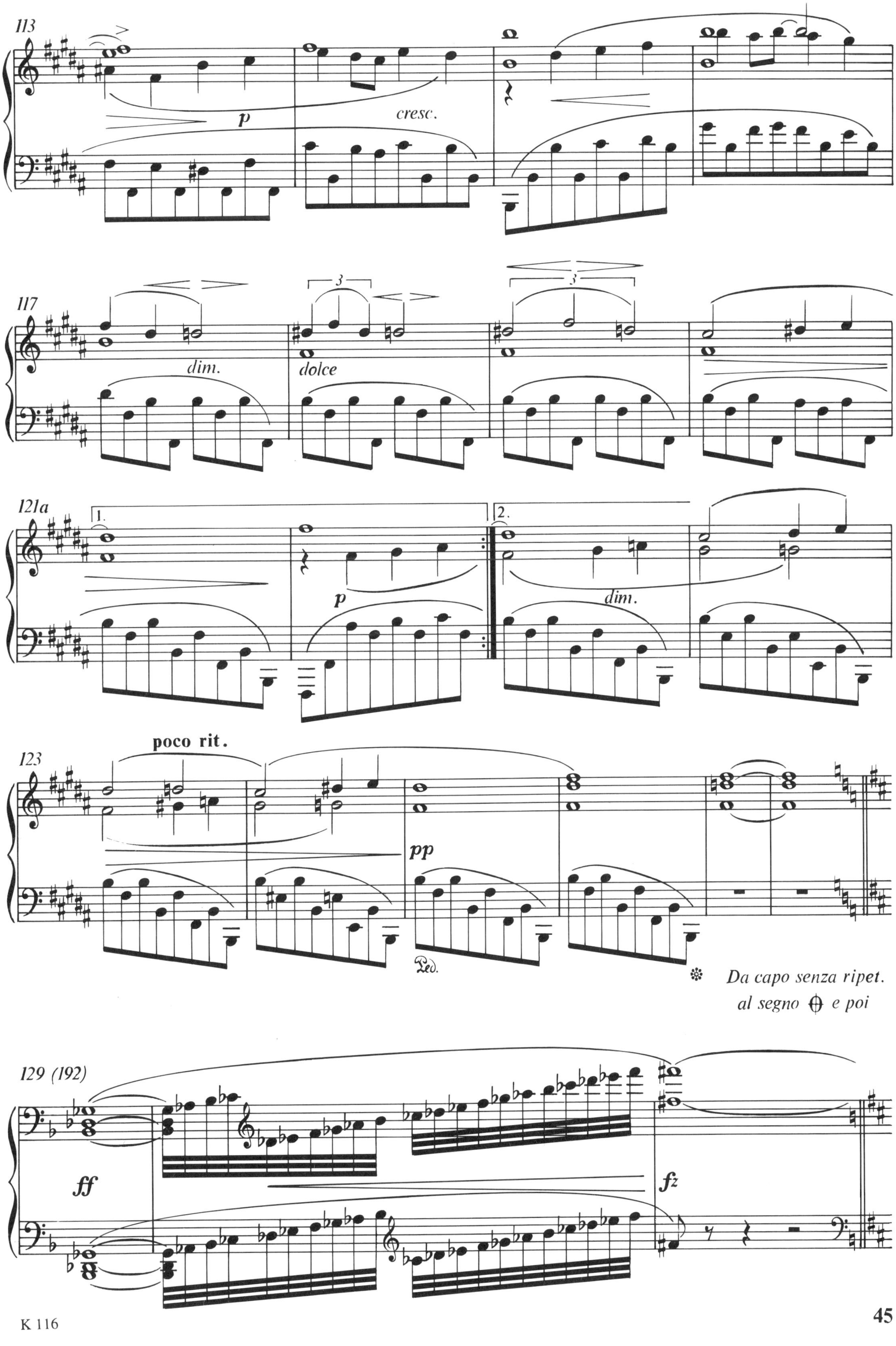
113
p
cresc.
117
dim.
dolce
3
3
121a
1.
2.
p
dim.
123
poco rit.
pp
Ped.
Da capo senza ripet.
al segno e poi
129 (192)
ff
fz

132 (195)
136 (199)
f
cresc.
140 (203)
8
f
144 (207)
più f
148 (211)
8
8
sf

152 (215)
fp
p
157 (220)
leggiero
pp
161 (224)
164 (227)
poco a
dim. poco a poco
167 (230)
poco ri - - tar - - dan - - do - -
pp
Ped.

Op. 79, No. 2

Molto passionato, ma non troppo allegro
2.
m. s.
m. s.
f
3
rit. - - - - - - in tempo
6
rit. - - - - - - in
f
9
tempo
f
12
mp

15
18
cresc.
p mezza
f
21
voce
24
27
cre
scen
do
30
f
8

33
m. s.
m. s.
m. s.
m. s.
36
m. s.
m. s.
m. s.
p
Ped.
39
m. s.
p
42
45
p
Ped.
48
dim.

51
p mezza voce
54
57
ff
60
p
ff
63
m. s.
p dim.
ppp
sotto voce
col Ped.
66

69
72
75
78
ff
p
81
pp
ri - te - nu - to
lunga
in tempo
84
dim.
f
m. s.
Ped.

rit. - - - - - in tempo
87
m. s.
90
rit. - - - - - - in tempo
93
f
96
f
mp
99
102
cresc.

105
p mezza voce
107
f
110
cresc.
113
ff
116
ff
p
dim.
(quasi rit.)
119
pp
ff

Dr. Eduard Hanslick gewidmet

16 Walzer

Originalfassung – Original Version – Version originale

Op. 39
Wien, 1865

Op. 39, No. 2

Op. 39, No. 3

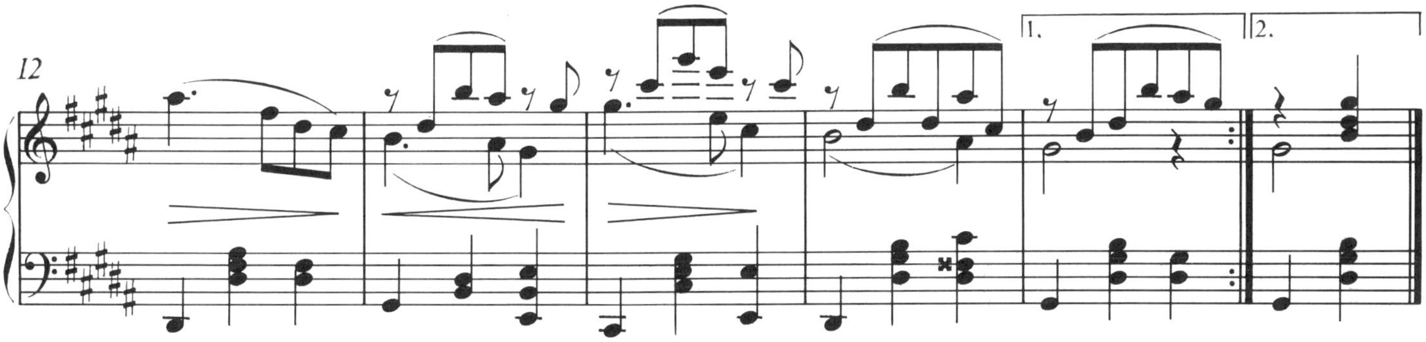

Op. 39, No. 4

Poco sostenuto

4.

Op. 39, No. 5

Grazioso

5.

Vivace

Op. 39, No. 6

6.

12
17
fp
22
27
cresc.
32
1.
2.
f
fp
fp
f
sf
sf

Poco più Andante
7.
p dolce
1.
2.
pp legato
Ped.
col Ped.
p
cresc. poco a
poco
ben legato
f
p

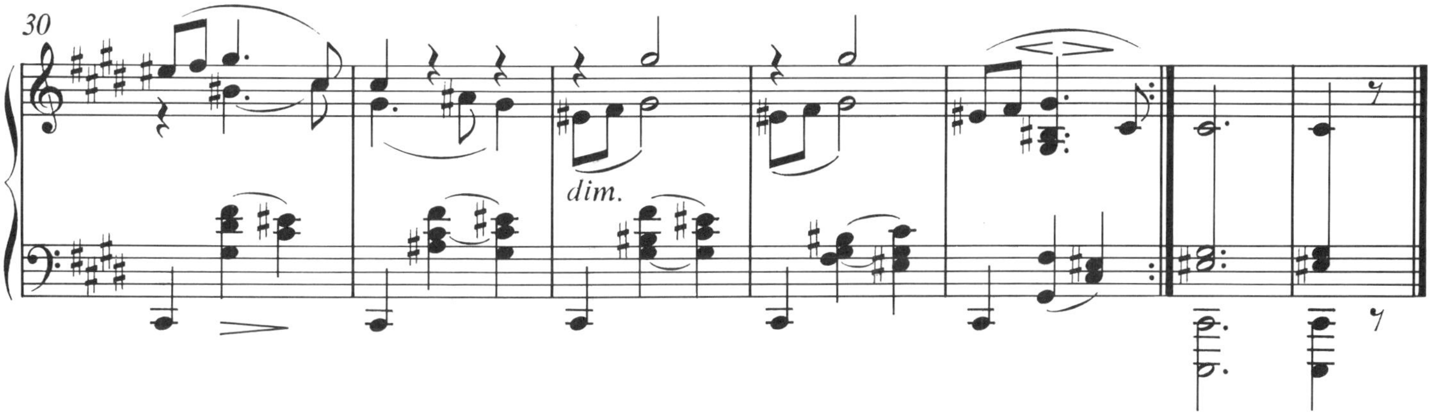

Op. 39, No. 8

8.

Op. 39, No. 9

9.

Op. 39, No. 10

10.

Op. 39, No. 11

Op. 39, No. 12

12.

espr. legato
p
cresc.
8
f
1.
2.
13
p
più dolce dim.
20
legato
cresc.
27
f
Ped.

Op. 39, No. 13

Op. 39, No. 14

13
dolce
18
cresc.
[>]
23
f
f
27
cresc.
32
f marcato

15.

Op. 39, No. 16

16.

Dr. Eduard Hanslick gewidmet

16 Walzer

Erleichterte Fassung – Facilitated Version – Version facilitée

Op. 39
Wien, 1865

Op. 39, No. 2

2.

Op. 39, No. 3

3.

Op. 39, No. 4

4. **Poco sostenuto**

Op. 39, No. 5

Grazioso

Vivace

Op. 39, No. 6

12
17
fp staccato
22
27
cresc.
32
1.
2.
f fp
fp
f sf
sf

Poco più Andante Op. 39, No. 7

7.

Op. 39, No. 8

8.

Op. 39, No. 9

9.

Op. 39, No. 10

10.

11.
fp
7
p
14
p
p
21
più legato
fp
28
dim.
35
p dolce
1.
2.

Op. 39, No. 12

12.
p
espr. legato
cresc.
8
f
1.
2.
13
più dolce
dim.
20
legato
cresc.
27
f

Op. 39, No. 13

13.

Op. 39, No. 14

14.

13
dolce
18
cresc.
23
f
f
27
cresc.
32
f marcato

15.

Op. 39, No. 16

10 Ungarische Tänze
Hungarian Dances – Danses Hongroises

WoO 1
1872

WoO 1, No. 1

25
mf
8
sf
Ped.
31
37
43
49
p leggiero
55
rf
f

p leggiero
col. Ped.
sf
p
f
Ossia (Brahms):
rit.

93
leggiero
8
p
p
101
p leggiero
espr.
109
8
p
p
117
8
mf
sf
123
sf

p leggiero
rf
p
rf
f
p leggiero
col. Ped.
sf
p
Ped.
sf
f
f
f
f

Allegro non assai
2.
f
sf
7
sf
sempre con passione
13
poco rit.
Vivace
sf
mf
19
sf
mf
poco sost.
p
Ped.
26
dolce
rit.
dim.
Ped.

33
in tempo
f
sf
38
sf
43
poco rit.
rit.
49
in tempo
p
cresc.
f
57
p
ten.
leggiero
Ped.
64
ten.
leggiero
cresc.
ten.
leggiero
Ped.
Ped.

69
f
p
leggiero
76
f
p
83
f
rit.
89
f
sf
sf
96
sempre con passione
poco rit.

103
Vivace
sf
mf
sf
110
mf
poco sost.
p
Ped.
dolce
117
rit.
Ped.
dim.
in tempo
f
123
sf
sf
129
cresc.
136
f
f

WoO 1, No. 3

25
sotto voce
29
p
33
cresc.
Vivace
37
ff
8
6
43
sf
Ossia (Brahms):

49
p
Ped.
52
sf
sf
rall. poco - - - - - - - a -
55
più p

poco
58
Tempo I
61
p grazioso
65
69
p

4.
Poco sostenuto
la melodia f ed espressivo
trem.
Ped.
sost.
rit.
molto cresc.
p
tempo molto animato
sfp
leggiero
cresc.
e string

Vivace
f ben marcato
mf passionato
m.d.
Ped.
[m.d.]
Fine

Molto allegro
66
p
pp sempre, ma ben marcato
legg.
Ped. Ped. Ped. Ped.
72
1.
2.
pp
76
cresc. poco a poco
81
sf

86
f sempre cresc. e string.
92
sf
98
ff
sf
104
p dim. e poco meno presto
sf
110
pp
dim. poco rit.
Da Capo sin' al Fine

WoO 1, No. 5

28
33
f marc.
38
poco rit.
44
in tempo
49
Vivace

55
poco rit.
in tempo
poco rit.
p
p leggiero
60
[in tempo]
poco rit.
p leggiero
p
65
[in tempo]
poco rit.
[in tempo]
p leggiero
dolce
p leggiero
70
f passionato
sf
sf
sf
sf
75
sf
sf

K 116

f marc.
poco rit.
in tempo

WoO 1, No. 6

6.
Vivace
poco sostenuto
tr
f
sf
p
8
più rit.
vivo in tempo
15
22
29
p leggiero

Molto sostenuto
sostenuto
ad lib.
p legg. ma marcato

poco sostenuto
più rit.
vivo in tempo
sempre vivace
sempre p e leggiero

94
100
106
112
p leggiero
117

WoO 1, No. 7

Allegretto vivace
molto sostenuto poco a poco - - - - - in tempo
7.
p
sf
f
6
molto sost. poco a poco - - - -
p
11
- - - - in tempo
sf
f
p
16
f
21
sf
rit.
molto sostenuto poco a
p

poco
in tempo
ad lib.
poco rit.
molto sost. poco a poco-
in tempo
poco rit.
vivo

Presto WoO 1, No. 8

31
37
f
cresc.
6
sf
sf
43
sfp
ff
49
f
sf
p leggiero
3
3
54
f
f
f
sf
p leggiero
Ped.
Ped.
8
60
8
sf
5

sempre
cresc.
ossia (Brahms):
leggiero

ben marc.
cresc.
glissando

116
ben marc.
cresc.
8
f
[7]
5
121
sf pp
Ped.
127
cresc. poco a poco
133
f
cresc.
6
sf
139
sfp
ff

145
pp legato
150
sempre
pp
155
sf
160
rit.
165
sf
f

Allegro
9.
f
tr
fp
3
7
f marcato
[>]
13
fp
f
molto p ma ben marcato
8
19
Poco sostenuto
25
p dolce
rit.
sf

rit.
in tempo
marcato
marcato
marcato
tr
molto p
pp
pp
Ped.

WoO 1, No. 10

10.
Presto
f
sf
sf
sf
Ped.
f
sf
p
f
sf
p
sf
p
sf
p
p
poco sost.
in tempo
p
poco sost.

31
in tempo
f
sf
p
37
sf
sf
42
p
47
f ben marcato
53
58

K 116

Gavotte

WoO posth. 3, No. 1
Düsseldorf, 1854–55

2 Gigues

WoO posth. 4
Düsseldorf, 1855

WoO posth. 4, No. 1

23
27
31
35
38
41

WoO posth. 4, No. 2

19
22
25
28
31
34
37

2 Sarabanden

WoO posth. 5
Düsseldorf, 1854–55

WoO posth. 5, No. 1

2.
f
p
5
cresc.
f
9
f
cresc.
14
f
19
cresc.
f

Appendix

Gavotte

WoO posth. 3, No. 2
Düsseldorf, 1854–55

23
f
cresc.
f
28
sf
sf
33
p
p
ff
ff
37
p
p
41
dim.
dim.
pp dim.
pp dim.

Notes

This edition is based upon the autographs of the piano works of Brahms and/or copies of first editions published during the composer's lifetime, most being Handexemplar copies (composer's printed copy) owned by the composer, which contain his subsequent revisions.

The editors have attempted to present a score whose appearance corresponds as closely as possible in content and form to the intentions of the composer. Unavoidable editorial additions have therefore been given in small print and in square brackets. Exceptions are some accidentals and changes of clef which have been added in the interests of musical legibility. Markings not in the autograph but added by Brahms during the preparation of the first edition, or added to the Handexemplar, have also been included. However, reference to these is made at the relevant place in the critical notes, and to all alternative readings arising in the sources.

Amendments based upon analogy have only been made when obvious slips of the pen have been corrected. The fingering given here strictly follows Brahms's own, and no suggestions have been given regarding performance or the execution of ornaments.

In cases where the sources contain important contradictions, the variants found in the composer's "Handexemplar" copy have been taken as authoritative. In the case of the Scherzo (Op. 4) and the set of Waltzes (Op. 39), where composer's revisions are not to be found in the Handexemplar copies, this procedure has been abandoned; instead decisions have been made according to particular instances (see the detailed notes below).

Scherzo Op. 4

Sources:

A: Autograph manuscript (Stichvorlage [engraver's copy] – Leipzig, Staatsarchiv), photocopy (Österreichische Nationalbibliothek, Musiksammlung, PhA 274).

B: Handexemplar (composer's printed copy) of the first edition of 1854 (Breitkopf und Härtel, Leipzig, plate number 8836), a copy without autograph alterations (Gesellschaft der Musikfreunde, Wien, Nachlass Brahms).

The autograph manuscript was prepared as the engraver's copy for the first edition, but differs in places (e.g. tempo markings) from the printed score. Since the Handexemplar contains no subsequent revisions, the two sources have been taken as equally valid.

Bar

1 lower stave: in **A** 1st quaver of upbeat d^1, similarly in bars 2 and 4; in **B** altered to b^1.
185: in **B** > written in both staves.
328-330 upper stave: according to **B** the slur is: 
Version in **A** followed here.
326-336 and 354-357 lower stave: slurs missing in **A**.
354: **A** has no *f*.
404: in **A** first chord is  with a faded staccato mark. Here the Handexemplar version is given.
534 lower stave: first chord (c–c^1) given as in **A**, and by analogy with bars 69-76. **B** has c–*e flat*–g–c^1.
596: *poco a poco accel.* only in **B**.
604: *Più mosso* only in **B**.
617: *Più sostenuto* only in **B**.

4 Balladen Op. 10

Sources:

A: Composer's Handexemplar of the first edition of 1856 (Breitkopf und Härtel, Leipzig, plate number 9226), copy revised by the composer (Gesellschaft der Musikfreunde, Wien, Nachlass Brahms).

B: Composer's Handexemplar of the composite volume published in 1875 (Breitkopf und Härtel, Leipzig, plate number 13598), copy revised by the composer (Gesellschaft der Musikfreunde, Wien, Nachlass Luithlen-Kalbeck VII 41553).

No manuscript survives of the Ballads, hence the early editions have to be taken as authentic sources. The first editions, including the revisions, were not considered by Brahms, it seems, to be the final version. In a letter to his new publisher, Simrock, he spoke of the need for revision, and opportunities for this (letter dated 14.3.1888), but it did not take place. ("Nach meinem Brief legte ich den Hartelschen Klavierband aufs Pult und spielte. Es wäre ein Unsinn, wenn ich anfangen wollte zu kritzeln! Ein paar Druckfehler sind drin, die können heraus, aber alles Schlimmer müssen wir schon drin lassen.")

Op. 10, No. 1

27: Tempo marking originally *Doppio movimento.* The composer changed it on the advice of R. Schumann.
29 lower stave: dot missing in sources from dotted minim in middle voice.

Op. 10, No. 3

76 upper stave: in **A** second chord is a^1–*c sharp*^{2}–*f sharp*^{2}, in **B** altered in pencil to a^1–*d sharp*^{2}–*f sharp*^{2}.

Op. 10, No. 4

47: in the sources ***pp*** is under 3rd beat last triplet quaver.
53 upper stave: last crotchet upward stem based on autograph revision in **A**.
54^a, 54^b and 64 upper stave: dot added to minim editorial.
57 upper stave: last crotchet downward stem editorial addition.
83 lower stave: 5th quaver *d* (with a natural sign) in the sources.
135: in the sources *mezza voce* only on 3rd beat.
137-138: $<$ given following **B**. In **A** crescendo marks printed separately in each bar, though in different staves (cf. bars 63-64).
138: in **A** ***p*** only on last quaver.
142 and 144 upper stave: last group has the (erroneous) rhythm  in the sources.

2 Rhapsodien Op. 79

Source:

A: Composer's Handexemplar of the first edition of 1880 (N. Simrock, Berlin, plate number 8166), copy revised by the composer (Gesellschaft der Musikfreunde, Wien, Nachlass Brahms).

No autograph survives of these pieces. The engraver's copy prepared for the first edition differs in large measure from the later published score, and thus hardly counts as a reliable source.
It is interesting to note that at the suggestion of the dedicatee, Elizabeth von Herzogenberg, Brahms, though at first reluctant, changed the genre title of the pieces from Klavierstücke to Rhapsodien.

Op. 79, No. 1

43: in the source originally *m.v.*
47 upper stave: flat missing in the source before the *e flat* in the 2nd chord.
82 and 147 lower stave: no 𝄾 in the source on 1st and 3rd beats.
129: the repeat written out in the source here abbreviated with *Da Capo* marking.

Op. 79, No. 2

In the following cases the supply of missing signs in justified by analogy:
1-8: articulation (based on 86-93);
25-26 and 54-55: articulation (based on 21-22);
91: 4th beat ***f*** (as in bar 6).

16 Walzer Op. 39, original version

Sources:

A: Engraver's copy for the first edition (Lund, Universitetsbiblioteket, Sammlung Taussig).
B: Composer's Handexemplar of the first edition of 1867 (J. Rieter-Biedermann, Leipzig und Winterthur, plate number 524), copy without composer's revisions (Gesellschaft der Musikfreunde, Wien, Nachlass Brahms).

As subsidiary sources, use has been made of the sources for the *Erleichterte Fassung* (see later), together with the engraver's copy of the four-hand version, and its edition of 1866 (J. Rieter-Biedermann, Leipzig und Winterthur, plate number 470).

Op. 39, No. 1

13-15 upper stave: slurs missing in **A**.
15-16: fingering found only in **A**.
16 upper stave: grace note *c sharp*^{3} joined to lower note in **B**, in other sources to upper note.

Op. 39, No. 2

7 lower stave: arpeggio on first beat missing in **A**. Here **B** followed.
13-14 lower stave: tie between *a sharp–a sharp* only in **B**.
19-20: <> found in **B**.
20-22 lower stave: arpeggios missing in **B** (cf. bars 4-6), in **A** only found in bar 20.

Op. 39, No. 3

8^b *lower stave:* legato slur missing in **A**.

Op. 39, No. 4

11 upper stave: 5th quaver in **A** e^1, in **B** and sources of arrangements d^1.
14 upper stave: > marks missing in **A**.
13, 15 upper stave: fingering given based on sources for the *Erleichterte Fassung.*
18: position of *cresc.* follows **B**.
21, 22: **A** has ***sf*** on 3rd crotchet. Here ***rf*** based on **B**.
26 lower stave: staccato on 3rd crotchet follows **B**, not found in **A**.

Op. 39, No. 5

16, 17: **A** has > on 3rd crotchet, here version in **B** given.

Op. 39, No. 6

3, 4, 7: Quavers in middle voice have staccato dots in **A**.
21 lower stave: 1st crotchet in **A** has *G sharp* grace note, not found in **B** or other versions.
30-32 lower stave: arpeggio on 3rd crotchet follows **A**.

Op. 39, No. 7

1 and analogous bars lower stave: tie between 2nd and 3rd crotchets missing in **A**. Here taken from **B**.
12 upper stave: > mark on 6th quaver taken from **A**.
29, 31, 32 lower stave: ties given following bar 32 of source **B** for the *Erleichterte Fassung.*

Op. 39, No. 8

8, 9 lower stave: staccatos missing in **A**. Given following **B**.
8-10: <> missing in **A**. Given following **B**.
12-13 upper stave: tie joining *f–f* missing in **A**. Given following **B** and analogous beginning of the piece.

Op. 39, No. 9

23^b: no dynamic mark in **A**, here given following other sources.

Op. 39, No. 10

11 upper stave: in **A** 2nd quaver is a third *a^1–c^2*, in **B** *a^1–c sharp^2*. Here corrected to *a sharp^1–c sharp^2* based on sources for the *Erleichterte Fassung* and the four-hand version.
16^a upper stave: tie joining *g^1–g^1* missing in **B**.
16^a and 16^b: > missing in **A**.

Op. 39, No. 11

9 upper stave: articulation follows **A.**

Op. 39, No. 14

18-19, 20-21 upper stave: legato slurs joining these bars missing in **A**.
22 lower stave: > mark on 5th quaver taken from sources for the four-hand version.
33, 34 upper stave: > marks missing in **A**.

Op. 39, No. 15

29 upper stave: 1st chord in **B** *e flat^2–c^3*. Here version in **A** given.
32-33, 33-34: the <> marks between these bars only in **B**.

Op. 39, No. 16

10 lower stave: arpeggio on 3rd crotchet taken from the sources for the *Erleichterte Fassung.*
18, 20 lower stave: staccato on 3rd crotchet missing in **B**. Given following source **A**.

16 Walzer Op. 39, facilitated version

Sources:

A: Engraver's copy for the first edition (Lund, Universitetsbiblioteket, Sammlung Taussig).
B: The first edition of 1867 (J. Rieter-Biedermann, Leipzig und Winterthur, plate number 525).

The composer sent his publisher immediately two versions of the Op. 39 waltzes "eine für vernünftige Hände und eine – vielleicht für die schöneren" (letter dated 7th February 1867).

Op. 39, No. 1

12, 16: grace note slurs based on **A**.
14: *cresc.* missing in **A**.

Op. 39, No. 2

9: *dolce* missing in **A**.
11 lower stave: fingering taken from **A**.
17: pedal marking only in **A**. Here – as in **B** – omitted.

Op. 39, No. 3

1: *dolce* missing in **A**.
13, 14 upper stave: legato slurs in **A**: 

16 upper stave: legato slur on 3rd crotchet missing in **A**.

Op. 39, No. 4

8: *decresc.* mark missing in **A**.
11 upper stave: in **A** 5th quaver *e^1*, probably an error. Corrected based on the other sources.
13: *più **f*** missing in **A**.
14: in **A** *cresc.* appears earlier, in bar 12.
18-21 lower stave: > marks missing in **A**. Here taken from the other sources.
21, 22: ***rf*** missing in **A**. Given based on the other sources.

Op. 39, No. 6

31: in source **A** for both two-hand versions the *cresc.* mark stretches from bar 31 to bar 32.

Op. 39, No. 7

1 and analogous bars lower stave: in **A** ties are occasionally missing. Given based on **B**.
23, 29, 31 and 33 lower stave: ties follow musical context, though not found in sources except bar 32 of *Erleichterte Fassung* (**B**).
25 upper stave: in **A** legato slur lasts for whole bar.
26: **A** has ***f*** *espress. cresc.* instead of *ben legato.* Here given following **B** and the sources for the original version.

Op. 39, No. 9

7: dynamic mark in **A**: <> Here given as in **B** and sources for original version.

Op. 39, No. 11

21: *più legato* missing in **A**. Given here following the other sources.

Op. 39, No. 12

2-3 upper stave: legato slur missing in **A**, supplied from other sources.
11-12 lower stave: tie missing in **A**.

Op. 39, No. 13

9: ***f*** on upbeat missing in **A**.

Op. 39, No. 14

22 lower stave: > mark on 5th quaver supplied from sources for four-hand version.
28, 32 upper stave: > marks only found in **B**.
33, 34 lower stave: > marks given following **B**.

Op. 39, No. 15

22: ***p*** only in **B**.
32-35: <> only found in source **B**.

Op. 39, No. 16

1: *cresc.* mark on upbeat only found in **B**.
9: ***p*** only in **B**.
9 lower stave: arpeggio on 3rd crotchet missing in **A** and **B**. Supplied from sources for original version.
9-10 lower stave: legato slur in middle voice repeated bar by bar in **A**.

10 Ungarische Tänze WoO 1

Sources:

A: First edition (N. Simrock, Berlin, 1872, plate numbers 7196, 7197), composer's Handexemplar without revisions (Gesellschaft der Musikfreunde, Wien, VII 28860).

As a subsidiary source the first edition of the four-hand version has also been consulted (N. Simrock, Berlin, 1869, plate numbers 336, 337).

It was not by accident that the composer added "gesetzt von J. Brahms" to the title of the Hungarian Dances, which bear no opus number, instead of "komponieret von". The pieces in the set are for the most part paraphrases of dances in one of the favourite csárdás collections of the period, the volume by Bartalus and Füredi: 101 Folk and Hungarian songs. The volume of csárdás melodies in Brahms's estate contains many marked passages, and on the evidence of concert programmes Brahms and Clara Schumann often improvised on these Hungarian tunes years before they appeared in print.

WoO 1, No. 2

33: the *in tempo* marking refers to the opening tempo, and not to the previous *vivace.* The same applies to bar 89, where there is no tempo marking.

WoO 1, No. 3

28, 29: missing staccatos supplied based on analogous bars and the four-hand version.

WoO 1, No. 5

61, 65 and 69: *in tempo* missing in the source. Supplied by analogy with bar 57.

WoO 1, No. 6

5, 9 and analogous bars upper stave: the slur on the grace notes in **A**: 

WoO 1, No. 7

5 and analogous bars, lower and upper staves: staccato dots on 1st quaver occasionally missing. Supplemented here only in bar 48, upper staff.

WoO 1, No. 8

1-8: in four-hand version slurs on each bar, as here in bars 25 ff and 65 ff.
59: in **A** 2nd semiquaver of 2nd beat a third d^3–f^3.
79 lower stave: the sources have ***f***, probably an error. Here changed to ***sf*** following analogous bars.
99, 107 and analogous bars upper stave: staccato on 1st quaver supplied based on four-hand version.
114 lower and upper staves: the markings *11* and *13* not in sources.
116 lower stave: fingering of fourth quaver triplet (2) probably an error, here given based on bar 108.
119 lower stave: the marking *7* not in the source. Possible alternative rhythm: 

WoO 1, No. 10

59-60 lower stave: tie joining *G–G* editorial.

Short dances, Op. posth.

The short dances dating from 1854-55 were probably intended by the composer as part of two planned suites (in A minor and B minor).

Gavotte WoO posth. 3, No. 1

Source:

Autograph (Robert Schumann-Haus, Zwickau) photocopy (Österreichische Nationalbibliothek PhA 266)

2 Gigues WoO posth. 4

Source:

Autograph (The Library of Congress, Whittall Foundation), a copy (Wiener Stadt- und Landesbibliothek, Musiksammlung MH 9016/c).

No. 1

last bar lower stave: last four notes crossed out, originally: 
The revised version given here.

No. 2

In the manuscript a thin line has been drawn through the 2nd Gigue by the composer.
16 upper stave upper part: no natural sign before 11th quaver in the source.
37 upper stave upper part: no natural sign before 10th quaver in the source.

2 Sarabande WoO posth. 5

No. 1

Sources:

A: Autograph 1 (Robert Schumann-Haus, Zwickau), a photocopy (Österreichische Nationalbibliothek, PhA 266)

B: Autograph 2, facsimile copy as supplement to posthumous first edition (J. Brahms: Zwei Sarabanden, Deutsche Brahms Gesellschaft 8, Berlin 1927).

No. 2

Sources:

A: Autograph 1 (The Library of Congress, Whittall Foundation), a copy (Wiener Stadt- und Landesbibliothek, Musiksammlung MH 9016/c).

B: Autograph 2 – v. No. 1.

Sources **A** and **B** for the two Sarabandes display important divergences. Since from every point of view source **B** appears to be a more final, complete, clarified version, it has been taken as the basis for this edition.

APPENDIX

Gavotte WoO 3, No. 2 (fragment)

In contradiction to our editorial principles – to publish only complete pieces – the bars of the 2nd Gavotte are issued here in a completed form. The piece is found together with WoO post. 3 No. 1 Gavotte and WoO post. 5 No. 1 Sarabande in the source ÖNB PhA 266. The manuscript breaks off at bar 26. The musical material is found in a completed form in the second movement of the Op. 88 String Quintet (2nd Trio). The completion of the piano version is given based on this movement.

H-1093 Budapest, Közraktár utca 10.

K 116/2

Distributed worldwide by
Könemann Verlagsgesellschaft mbH, Bonner Str. 126.
D-50968 Köln

Responsible co-editor: István Máriássy
Production: Detlev Schaper
Cover design: Peter Feierabend
Technical editor: Dezső Varga

Engraved by Kottamester Bt., Budapest:
Zsuzsanna Gedai, Dénes Hárs, Edina Lakatos, Zsuzsanna Mák

Printed by Kossuth Printing House Co., Budapest
Printed in Hungary

ISBN 963 8303 29 8